MY NOTES FOR
MEAL SUCCESS!
A Planner for Meal Notes

@Journals&Notebooks

My Notes For Meal Success!

Groceries

Produce

Meat

MONDAY	TUESDAY	WEDNESDAY
BREAKFAST:	BREAKFAST:	BREAKFAST:
LUNCH:	LUNCH:	LUNCH:
DINNER:	DINNER:	DINNER:
SNACKS:	SNACKS:	SNACKS:

My Notes For Meal Success!

THURSDAY	FRIDAY	SATURDAY	SUNDAY
BREAKFAST:	BREAKFAST:	BREAKFAST:	BREAKFAST:
LUNCH:	LUNCH:	LUNCH:	LUNCH:
DINNER:	DINNER:	DINNER:	DINNER:
SNACKS:	SNACKS:	SNACKS:	SNACKS:

NOTES:

My Notes For Meal Success!

Groceries

Produce

Meat

MONDAY	TUESDAY	WEDNESDAY
BREAKFAST:	BREAKFAST:	BREAKFAST:
LUNCH:	LUNCH:	LUNCH:
DINNER:	DINNER:	DINNER:
SNACKS:	SNACKS:	SNACKS:

My Notes For Meal Success!

THURSDAY	FRIDAY	SATURDAY	SUNDAY
BREAKFAST:	BREAKFAST:	BREAKFAST:	BREAKFAST:
LUNCH:	LUNCH:	LUNCH:	LUNCH:
DINNER:	DINNER:	DINNER:	DINNER:
SNACKS:	SNACKS:	SNACKS:	SNACKS:

NOTES:

My Notes For Meal Success!

Groceries

Produce

Meat

MONDAY	TUESDAY	WEDNESDAY
BREAKFAST:	BREAKFAST:	BREAKFAST:
LUNCH:	LUNCH:	LUNCH:
DINNER:	DINNER:	DINNER:
SNACKS:	SNACKS:	SNACKS:

My Notes For Meal Success!

THURSDAY	FRIDAY	SATURDAY	SUNDAY
BREAKFAST:	BREAKFAST:	BREAKFAST:	BREAKFAST:
LUNCH:	LUNCH:	LUNCH:	LUNCH:
DINNER:	DINNER:	DINNER:	DINNER:
SNACKS:	SNACKS:	SNACKS:	SNACKS:

NOTES:

My Notes For Meal Success!

Groceries

Produce

Meat

MONDAY	TUESDAY	WEDNESDAY
BREAKFAST:	BREAKFAST:	BREAKFAST:
LUNCH:	LUNCH:	LUNCH:
DINNER:	DINNER:	DINNER:
SNACKS:	SNACKS:	SNACKS:

My Notes For Meal Success!

THURSDAY	FRIDAY	SATURDAY	SUNDAY
BREAKFAST:	BREAKFAST:	BREAKFAST:	BREAKFAST:
LUNCH:	LUNCH:	LUNCH:	LUNCH:
DINNER:	DINNER:	DINNER:	DINNER:
SNACKS:	SNACKS:	SNACKS:	SNACKS:

NOTES:

My Notes For Meal Success!

Groceries

Produce

Meat

MONDAY	TUESDAY	WEDNESDAY
BREAKFAST:	BREAKFAST:	BREAKFAST:
LUNCH:	LUNCH:	LUNCH:
DINNER:	DINNER:	DINNER:
SNACKS:	SNACKS:	SNACKS:

My Notes For Meal Success!

THURSDAY	FRIDAY	SATURDAY	SUNDAY
BREAKFAST:	BREAKFAST:	BREAKFAST:	BREAKFAST:
LUNCH:	LUNCH:	LUNCH:	LUNCH:
DINNER:	DINNER:	DINNER:	DINNER:
SNACKS:	SNACKS:	SNACKS:	SNACKS:

NOTES:

My Notes For Meal Success!

Groceries

Produce

Meat

MONDAY	TUESDAY	WEDNESDAY
BREAKFAST:	BREAKFAST:	BREAKFAST:
LUNCH:	LUNCH:	LUNCH:
DINNER:	DINNER:	DINNER:
SNACKS:	SNACKS:	SNACKS:

My Notes For Meal Success!

THURSDAY	FRIDAY	SATURDAY	SUNDAY
BREAKFAST:	BREAKFAST:	BREAKFAST:	BREAKFAST:
LUNCH:	LUNCH:	LUNCH:	LUNCH:
DINNER:	DINNER:	DINNER:	DINNER:
SNACKS:	SNACKS:	SNACKS:	SNACKS:

NOTES:

My Notes For Meal Success!

Groceries

Produce

Meat

MONDAY	TUESDAY	WEDNESDAY
BREAKFAST:	BREAKFAST:	BREAKFAST:
LUNCH:	LUNCH:	LUNCH:
DINNER:	DINNER:	DINNER:
SNACKS:	SNACKS:	SNACKS:

My Notes For Meal Success!

THURSDAY	FRIDAY	SATURDAY	SUNDAY
BREAKFAST:	BREAKFAST:	BREAKFAST:	BREAKFAST:
LUNCH:	LUNCH:	LUNCH:	LUNCH:
DINNER:	DINNER:	DINNER:	DINNER:
SNACKS:	SNACKS:	SNACKS:	SNACKS:

NOTES:

My Notes For Meal Success!

Groceries

Produce

Meat

MONDAY	TUESDAY	WEDNESDAY
BREAKFAST:	BREAKFAST:	BREAKFAST:
LUNCH:	LUNCH:	LUNCH:
DINNER:	DINNER:	DINNER:
SNACKS:	SNACKS:	SNACKS:

My Notes For Meal Success!

THURSDAY	FRIDAY	SATURDAY	SUNDAY
BREAKFAST:	BREAKFAST:	BREAKFAST:	BREAKFAST:
LUNCH:	LUNCH:	LUNCH:	LUNCH:
DINNER:	DINNER:	DINNER:	DINNER:
SNACKS:	SNACKS:	SNACKS:	SNACKS:

NOTES:

My Notes For Meal Success!

Groceries

Produce

Meat

MONDAY	TUESDAY	WEDNESDAY
BREAKFAST:	BREAKFAST:	BREAKFAST:
LUNCH:	LUNCH:	LUNCH:
DINNER:	DINNER:	DINNER:
SNACKS:	SNACKS:	SNACKS:

My Notes For Meal Success!

THURSDAY	FRIDAY	SATURDAY	SUNDAY
BREAKFAST:	BREAKFAST:	BREAKFAST:	BREAKFAST:
LUNCH:	LUNCH:	LUNCH:	LUNCH:
DINNER:	DINNER:	DINNER:	DINNER:
SNACKS:	SNACKS:	SNACKS:	SNACKS:

NOTES:

My Notes For Meal Success!

Groceries

Produce

Meat

MONDAY	TUESDAY	WEDNESDAY
BREAKFAST:	BREAKFAST:	BREAKFAST:
LUNCH:	LUNCH:	LUNCH:
DINNER:	DINNER:	DINNER:
SNACKS:	SNACKS:	SNACKS:

My Notes For Meal Success!

THURSDAY	FRIDAY	SATURDAY	SUNDAY
BREAKFAST:	BREAKFAST:	BREAKFAST:	BREAKFAST:
LUNCH:	LUNCH:	LUNCH:	LUNCH:
DINNER:	DINNER:	DINNER:	DINNER:
SNACKS:	SNACKS:	SNACKS:	SNACKS:

NOTES:

My Notes For Meal Success!

Groceries

Produce

Meat

MONDAY	TUESDAY	WEDNESDAY
BREAKFAST:	BREAKFAST:	BREAKFAST:
LUNCH:	LUNCH:	LUNCH:
DINNER:	DINNER:	DINNER:
SNACKS:	SNACKS:	SNACKS:

My Notes For Meal Success!

THURSDAY	FRIDAY	SATURDAY	SUNDAY
BREAKFAST:	BREAKFAST:	BREAKFAST:	BREAKFAST:
LUNCH:	LUNCH:	LUNCH:	LUNCH:
DINNER:	DINNER:	DINNER:	DINNER:
SNACKS:	SNACKS:	SNACKS:	SNACKS:

NOTES:

My Notes For Meal Success!

Groceries

Produce

Meat

MONDAY	TUESDAY	WEDNESDAY
BREAKFAST:	BREAKFAST:	BREAKFAST:
LUNCH:	LUNCH:	LUNCH:
DINNER:	DINNER:	DINNER:
SNACKS:	SNACKS:	SNACKS:

My Notes For Meal Success!

THURSDAY	FRIDAY	SATURDAY	SUNDAY
BREAKFAST:	BREAKFAST:	BREAKFAST:	BREAKFAST:
LUNCH:	LUNCH:	LUNCH:	LUNCH:
DINNER:	DINNER:	DINNER:	DINNER:
SNACKS:	SNACKS:	SNACKS:	SNACKS:

NOTES:

My Notes For Meal Success!

Groceries

Produce

Meat

MONDAY	TUESDAY	WEDNESDAY
BREAKFAST:	BREAKFAST:	BREAKFAST:
LUNCH:	LUNCH:	LUNCH:
DINNER:	DINNER:	DINNER:
SNACKS:	SNACKS:	SNACKS:

My Notes For Meal Success!

THURSDAY	FRIDAY	SATURDAY	SUNDAY
BREAKFAST:	BREAKFAST:	BREAKFAST:	BREAKFAST:
LUNCH:	LUNCH:	LUNCH:	LUNCH:
DINNER:	DINNER:	DINNER:	DINNER:
SNACKS:	SNACKS:	SNACKS:	SNACKS:

NOTES:

My Notes For Meal Success!

Groceries

Produce

Meat

MONDAY	TUESDAY	WEDNESDAY
BREAKFAST:	BREAKFAST:	BREAKFAST:
LUNCH:	LUNCH:	LUNCH:
DINNER:	DINNER:	DINNER:
SNACKS:	SNACKS:	SNACKS:

My Notes For Meal Success!

THURSDAY	FRIDAY	SATURDAY	SUNDAY
BREAKFAST:	BREAKFAST:	BREAKFAST:	BREAKFAST:
LUNCH:	LUNCH:	LUNCH:	LUNCH:
DINNER:	DINNER:	DINNER:	DINNER:
SNACKS:	SNACKS:	SNACKS:	SNACKS:

NOTES:

My Notes For Meal Success!

Groceries

Produce

Meat

MONDAY	TUESDAY	WEDNESDAY
BREAKFAST:	BREAKFAST:	BREAKFAST:
LUNCH:	LUNCH:	LUNCH:
DINNER:	DINNER:	DINNER:
SNACKS:	SNACKS:	SNACKS:

My Notes For Meal Success!

THURSDAY	FRIDAY	SATURDAY	SUNDAY
BREAKFAST:	BREAKFAST:	BREAKFAST:	BREAKFAST:
LUNCH:	LUNCH:	LUNCH:	LUNCH:
DINNER:	DINNER:	DINNER:	DINNER:
SNACKS:	SNACKS:	SNACKS:	SNACKS:

NOTES:

My Notes For Meal Success!

Groceries

Produce

Meat

MONDAY	TUESDAY	WEDNESDAY
BREAKFAST:	BREAKFAST:	BREAKFAST:
LUNCH:	LUNCH:	LUNCH:
DINNER:	DINNER:	DINNER:
SNACKS:	SNACKS:	SNACKS:

My Notes For Meal Success!

THURSDAY	FRIDAY	SATURDAY	SUNDAY
BREAKFAST:	BREAKFAST:	BREAKFAST:	BREAKFAST:
LUNCH:	LUNCH:	LUNCH:	LUNCH:
DINNER:	DINNER:	DINNER:	DINNER:
SNACKS:	SNACKS:	SNACKS:	SNACKS:

NOTES:

My Notes For Meal Success!

Groceries

Produce

Meat

MONDAY	TUESDAY	WEDNESDAY
BREAKFAST:	BREAKFAST:	BREAKFAST:
LUNCH:	LUNCH:	LUNCH:
DINNER:	DINNER:	DINNER:
SNACKS:	SNACKS:	SNACKS:

My Notes For Meal Success!

THURSDAY	FRIDAY	SATURDAY	SUNDAY
BREAKFAST:	BREAKFAST:	BREAKFAST:	BREAKFAST:
LUNCH:	LUNCH:	LUNCH:	LUNCH:
DINNER:	DINNER:	DINNER:	DINNER:
SNACKS:	SNACKS:	SNACKS:	SNACKS:

NOTES:

My Notes For Meal Success!

Groceries

Produce

Meat

MONDAY	TUESDAY	WEDNESDAY
BREAKFAST:	BREAKFAST:	BREAKFAST:
LUNCH:	LUNCH:	LUNCH:
DINNER:	DINNER:	DINNER:
SNACKS:	SNACKS:	SNACKS:

My Notes For Meal Success!

THURSDAY	FRIDAY	SATURDAY	SUNDAY
BREAKFAST:	BREAKFAST:	BREAKFAST:	BREAKFAST:
LUNCH:	LUNCH:	LUNCH:	LUNCH:
DINNER:	DINNER:	DINNER:	DINNER:
SNACKS:	SNACKS:	SNACKS:	SNACKS:

NOTES:

My Notes For Meal Success!

Groceries

Produce

Meat

MONDAY	TUESDAY	WEDNESDAY
BREAKFAST:	BREAKFAST:	BREAKFAST:
LUNCH:	LUNCH:	LUNCH:
DINNER:	DINNER:	DINNER:
SNACKS:	SNACKS:	SNACKS:

My Notes For Meal Success!

THURSDAY	FRIDAY	SATURDAY	SUNDAY
BREAKFAST:	BREAKFAST:	BREAKFAST:	BREAKFAST:
LUNCH:	LUNCH:	LUNCH:	LUNCH:
DINNER:	DINNER:	DINNER:	DINNER:
SNACKS:	SNACKS:	SNACKS:	SNACKS:

NOTES:

My Notes For Meal Success!

Groceries

Produce

Meat

MONDAY	TUESDAY	WEDNESDAY
BREAKFAST:	BREAKFAST:	BREAKFAST:
LUNCH:	LUNCH:	LUNCH:
DINNER:	DINNER:	DINNER:
SNACKS:	SNACKS:	SNACKS:

My Notes For Meal Success!

THURSDAY	FRIDAY	SATURDAY	SUNDAY
BREAKFAST:	BREAKFAST:	BREAKFAST:	BREAKFAST:
LUNCH:	LUNCH:	LUNCH:	LUNCH:
DINNER:	DINNER:	DINNER:	DINNER:
SNACKS:	SNACKS:	SNACKS:	SNACKS:

NOTES:

My Notes For Meal Success!

Groceries

Produce

Meat

MONDAY	TUESDAY	WEDNESDAY
BREAKFAST:	BREAKFAST:	BREAKFAST:
LUNCH:	LUNCH:	LUNCH:
DINNER:	DINNER:	DINNER:
SNACKS:	SNACKS:	SNACKS:

My Notes For Meal Success!

THURSDAY	FRIDAY	SATURDAY	SUNDAY
BREAKFAST:	BREAKFAST:	BREAKFAST:	BREAKFAST:
LUNCH:	LUNCH:	LUNCH:	LUNCH:
DINNER:	DINNER:	DINNER:	DINNER:
SNACKS:	SNACKS:	SNACKS:	SNACKS:

NOTES:

My Notes For Meal Success!

Groceries

Produce

Meat

MONDAY	TUESDAY	WEDNESDAY
BREAKFAST:	BREAKFAST:	BREAKFAST:
LUNCH:	LUNCH:	LUNCH:
DINNER:	DINNER:	DINNER:
SNACKS:	SNACKS:	SNACKS:

My Notes For Meal Success!

THURSDAY	FRIDAY	SATURDAY	SUNDAY
BREAKFAST:	BREAKFAST:	BREAKFAST:	BREAKFAST:
LUNCH:	LUNCH:	LUNCH:	LUNCH:
DINNER:	DINNER:	DINNER:	DINNER:
SNACKS:	SNACKS:	SNACKS:	SNACKS:

NOTES:

My Notes For Meal Success!

Groceries

Produce

Meat

MONDAY	TUESDAY	WEDNESDAY
BREAKFAST:	BREAKFAST:	BREAKFAST:
LUNCH:	LUNCH:	LUNCH:
DINNER:	DINNER:	DINNER:
SNACKS:	SNACKS:	SNACKS:

My Notes For Meal Success!

THURSDAY	FRIDAY	SATURDAY	SUNDAY
BREAKFAST:	BREAKFAST:	BREAKFAST:	BREAKFAST:
LUNCH:	LUNCH:	LUNCH:	LUNCH:
DINNER:	DINNER:	DINNER:	DINNER:
SNACKS:	SNACKS:	SNACKS:	SNACKS:

NOTES:

My Notes For Meal Success!

Groceries

Produce

Meat

MONDAY	TUESDAY	WEDNESDAY
BREAKFAST:	BREAKFAST:	BREAKFAST:
LUNCH:	LUNCH:	LUNCH:
DINNER:	DINNER:	DINNER:
SNACKS:	SNACKS:	SNACKS:

My Notes For Meal Success!

THURSDAY	FRIDAY	SATURDAY	SUNDAY
BREAKFAST:	BREAKFAST:	BREAKFAST:	BREAKFAST:
LUNCH:	LUNCH:	LUNCH:	LUNCH:
DINNER:	DINNER:	DINNER:	DINNER:
SNACKS:	SNACKS:	SNACKS:	SNACKS:

NOTES:

My Notes For Meal Success!

Groceries

Produce

Meat

MONDAY	TUESDAY	WEDNESDAY
BREAKFAST:	BREAKFAST:	BREAKFAST:
LUNCH:	LUNCH:	LUNCH:
DINNER:	DINNER:	DINNER:
SNACKS:	SNACKS:	SNACKS:

My Notes For Meal Success!

THURSDAY	FRIDAY	SATURDAY	SUNDAY
BREAKFAST:	BREAKFAST:	BREAKFAST:	BREAKFAST:
LUNCH:	LUNCH:	LUNCH:	LUNCH:
DINNER:	DINNER:	DINNER:	DINNER:
SNACKS:	SNACKS:	SNACKS:	SNACKS:

NOTES:

My Notes For Meal Success!

Groceries

Produce

Meat

MONDAY	TUESDAY	WEDNESDAY
BREAKFAST:	BREAKFAST:	BREAKFAST:
LUNCH:	LUNCH:	LUNCH:
DINNER:	DINNER:	DINNER:
SNACKS:	SNACKS:	SNACKS:

My Notes For Meal Success!

THURSDAY	FRIDAY	SATURDAY	SUNDAY
BREAKFAST:	BREAKFAST:	BREAKFAST:	BREAKFAST:
LUNCH:	LUNCH:	LUNCH:	LUNCH:
DINNER:	DINNER:	DINNER:	DINNER:
SNACKS:	SNACKS:	SNACKS:	SNACKS:

NOTES:

My Notes For Meal Success!

Groceries

Produce

Meat

MONDAY	TUESDAY	WEDNESDAY
BREAKFAST:	BREAKFAST:	BREAKFAST:
LUNCH:	LUNCH:	LUNCH:
DINNER:	DINNER:	DINNER:
SNACKS:	SNACKS:	SNACKS:

My Notes For Meal Success!

THURSDAY	FRIDAY	SATURDAY	SUNDAY
BREAKFAST:	BREAKFAST:	BREAKFAST:	BREAKFAST:
LUNCH:	LUNCH:	LUNCH:	LUNCH:
DINNER:	DINNER:	DINNER:	DINNER:
SNACKS:	SNACKS:	SNACKS:	SNACKS:

NOTES:

My Notes For Meal Success!

Groceries

Produce

Meat

MONDAY	TUESDAY	WEDNESDAY
BREAKFAST:	BREAKFAST:	BREAKFAST:
LUNCH:	LUNCH:	LUNCH:
DINNER:	DINNER:	DINNER:
SNACKS:	SNACKS:	SNACKS:

My Notes For Meal Success!

THURSDAY	FRIDAY	SATURDAY	SUNDAY
BREAKFAST:	BREAKFAST:	BREAKFAST:	BREAKFAST:
LUNCH:	LUNCH:	LUNCH:	LUNCH:
DINNER:	DINNER:	DINNER:	DINNER:
SNACKS:	SNACKS:	SNACKS:	SNACKS:

NOTES:

My Notes For Meal Success!

Groceries

Produce

Meat

MONDAY	TUESDAY	WEDNESDAY
BREAKFAST:	BREAKFAST:	BREAKFAST:
LUNCH:	LUNCH:	LUNCH:
DINNER:	DINNER:	DINNER:
SNACKS:	SNACKS:	SNACKS:

My Notes For Meal Success!

THURSDAY	FRIDAY	SATURDAY	SUNDAY
BREAKFAST:	BREAKFAST:	BREAKFAST:	BREAKFAST:
LUNCH:	LUNCH:	LUNCH:	LUNCH:
DINNER:	DINNER:	DINNER:	DINNER:
SNACKS:	SNACKS:	SNACKS:	SNACKS:

NOTES:

My Notes For Meal Success!

Groceries

Produce

Meat

MONDAY	TUESDAY	WEDNESDAY
BREAKFAST:	BREAKFAST:	BREAKFAST:
LUNCH:	LUNCH:	LUNCH:
DINNER:	DINNER:	DINNER:
SNACKS:	SNACKS:	SNACKS:

My Notes For Meal Success!

THURSDAY	FRIDAY	SATURDAY	SUNDAY
BREAKFAST:	BREAKFAST:	BREAKFAST:	BREAKFAST:
LUNCH:	LUNCH:	LUNCH:	LUNCH:
DINNER:	DINNER:	DINNER:	DINNER:
SNACKS:	SNACKS:	SNACKS:	SNACKS:

NOTES:

My Notes For Meal Success!

Groceries

Produce

Meat

MONDAY	TUESDAY	WEDNESDAY
BREAKFAST:	BREAKFAST:	BREAKFAST:
LUNCH:	LUNCH:	LUNCH:
DINNER:	DINNER:	DINNER:
SNACKS:	SNACKS:	SNACKS:

My Notes For Meal Success!

THURSDAY	FRIDAY	SATURDAY	SUNDAY
BREAKFAST:	BREAKFAST:	BREAKFAST:	BREAKFAST:
LUNCH:	LUNCH:	LUNCH:	LUNCH:
DINNER:	DINNER:	DINNER:	DINNER:
SNACKS:	SNACKS:	SNACKS:	SNACKS:

NOTES:

My Notes For Meal Success!

Groceries

Produce

Meat

MONDAY	TUESDAY	WEDNESDAY
BREAKFAST:	BREAKFAST:	BREAKFAST:
LUNCH:	LUNCH:	LUNCH:
DINNER:	DINNER:	DINNER:
SNACKS:	SNACKS:	SNACKS:

My Notes For Meal Success!

THURSDAY	FRIDAY	SATURDAY	SUNDAY
BREAKFAST:	BREAKFAST:	BREAKFAST:	BREAKFAST:
LUNCH:	LUNCH:	LUNCH:	LUNCH:
DINNER:	DINNER:	DINNER:	DINNER:
SNACKS:	SNACKS:	SNACKS:	SNACKS:

NOTES:

My Notes For Meal Success!

Groceries

Produce

Meat

MONDAY	TUESDAY	WEDNESDAY
BREAKFAST:	BREAKFAST:	BREAKFAST:
LUNCH:	LUNCH:	LUNCH:
DINNER:	DINNER:	DINNER:
SNACKS:	SNACKS:	SNACKS:

My Notes For Meal Success!

THURSDAY	FRIDAY	SATURDAY	SUNDAY
BREAKFAST:	BREAKFAST:	BREAKFAST:	BREAKFAST:
LUNCH:	LUNCH:	LUNCH:	LUNCH:
DINNER:	DINNER:	DINNER:	DINNER:
SNACKS:	SNACKS:	SNACKS:	SNACKS:

NOTES:

My Notes For Meal Success!

Groceries

Produce

Meat

MONDAY	TUESDAY	WEDNESDAY
BREAKFAST:	BREAKFAST:	BREAKFAST:
LUNCH:	LUNCH:	LUNCH:
DINNER:	DINNER:	DINNER:
SNACKS:	SNACKS:	SNACKS:

My Notes For Meal Success!

THURSDAY	FRIDAY	SATURDAY	SUNDAY
BREAKFAST:	BREAKFAST:	BREAKFAST:	BREAKFAST:
LUNCH:	LUNCH:	LUNCH:	LUNCH:
DINNER:	DINNER:	DINNER:	DINNER:
SNACKS:	SNACKS:	SNACKS:	SNACKS:

NOTES:

My Notes For Meal Success!

Groceries

Produce

Meat

MONDAY	TUESDAY	WEDNESDAY
BREAKFAST:	BREAKFAST:	BREAKFAST:
LUNCH:	LUNCH:	LUNCH:
DINNER:	DINNER:	DINNER:
SNACKS:	SNACKS:	SNACKS:

My Notes For Meal Success!

THURSDAY	FRIDAY	SATURDAY	SUNDAY
BREAKFAST:	BREAKFAST:	BREAKFAST:	BREAKFAST:
LUNCH:	LUNCH:	LUNCH:	LUNCH:
DINNER:	DINNER:	DINNER:	DINNER:
SNACKS:	SNACKS:	SNACKS:	SNACKS:

NOTES:

My Notes For Meal Success!

Groceries

Produce

Meat

MONDAY	TUESDAY	WEDNESDAY
BREAKFAST:	BREAKFAST:	BREAKFAST:
LUNCH:	LUNCH:	LUNCH:
DINNER:	DINNER:	DINNER:
SNACKS:	SNACKS:	SNACKS:

My Notes For Meal Success!

THURSDAY	FRIDAY	SATURDAY	SUNDAY
BREAKFAST:	BREAKFAST:	BREAKFAST:	BREAKFAST:
LUNCH:	LUNCH:	LUNCH:	LUNCH:
DINNER:	DINNER:	DINNER:	DINNER:
SNACKS:	SNACKS:	SNACKS:	SNACKS:

NOTES:

My Notes For Meal Success!

Groceries

Produce

Meat

MONDAY	TUESDAY	WEDNESDAY
BREAKFAST:	BREAKFAST:	BREAKFAST:
LUNCH:	LUNCH:	LUNCH:
DINNER:	DINNER:	DINNER:
SNACKS:	SNACKS:	SNACKS:

My Notes For Meal Success!

THURSDAY	FRIDAY	SATURDAY	SUNDAY
BREAKFAST:	BREAKFAST:	BREAKFAST:	BREAKFAST:
LUNCH:	LUNCH:	LUNCH:	LUNCH:
DINNER:	DINNER:	DINNER:	DINNER:
SNACKS:	SNACKS:	SNACKS:	SNACKS:

NOTES:

My Notes For Meal Success!

Groceries

Produce

Meat

MONDAY	TUESDAY	WEDNESDAY
BREAKFAST:	BREAKFAST:	BREAKFAST:
LUNCH:	LUNCH:	LUNCH:
DINNER:	DINNER:	DINNER:
SNACKS:	SNACKS:	SNACKS:

My Notes For Meal Success!

THURSDAY	FRIDAY	SATURDAY	SUNDAY
BREAKFAST:	BREAKFAST:	BREAKFAST:	BREAKFAST:
LUNCH:	LUNCH:	LUNCH:	LUNCH:
DINNER:	DINNER:	DINNER:	DINNER:
SNACKS:	SNACKS:	SNACKS:	SNACKS:

NOTES:

My Notes For Meal Success!

Groceries

Produce

Meat

MONDAY	TUESDAY	WEDNESDAY
BREAKFAST:	BREAKFAST:	BREAKFAST:
LUNCH:	LUNCH:	LUNCH:
DINNER:	DINNER:	DINNER:
SNACKS:	SNACKS:	SNACKS:

My Notes For Meal Success!

THURSDAY	FRIDAY	SATURDAY	SUNDAY
BREAKFAST:	BREAKFAST:	BREAKFAST:	BREAKFAST:
LUNCH:	LUNCH:	LUNCH:	LUNCH:
DINNER:	DINNER:	DINNER:	DINNER:
SNACKS:	SNACKS:	SNACKS:	SNACKS:

NOTES:

My Notes For Meal Success!

Groceries

Produce

Meat

MONDAY	TUESDAY	WEDNESDAY
BREAKFAST:	BREAKFAST:	BREAKFAST:
LUNCH:	LUNCH:	LUNCH:
DINNER:	DINNER:	DINNER:
SNACKS:	SNACKS:	SNACKS:

My Notes For Meal Success!

THURSDAY	FRIDAY	SATURDAY	SUNDAY
BREAKFAST:	BREAKFAST:	BREAKFAST:	BREAKFAST:
LUNCH:	LUNCH:	LUNCH:	LUNCH:
DINNER:	DINNER:	DINNER:	DINNER:
SNACKS:	SNACKS:	SNACKS:	SNACKS:

NOTES:

My Notes For Meal Success!

Groceries

Produce

Meat

MONDAY	TUESDAY	WEDNESDAY
BREAKFAST:	BREAKFAST:	BREAKFAST:
LUNCH:	LUNCH:	LUNCH:
DINNER:	DINNER:	DINNER:
SNACKS:	SNACKS:	SNACKS:

My Notes For Meal Success!

THURSDAY	FRIDAY	SATURDAY	SUNDAY
BREAKFAST:	BREAKFAST:	BREAKFAST:	BREAKFAST:
LUNCH:	LUNCH:	LUNCH:	LUNCH:
DINNER:	DINNER:	DINNER:	DINNER:
SNACKS:	SNACKS:	SNACKS:	SNACKS:

NOTES:

My Notes For Meal Success!

Groceries

Produce

Meat

MONDAY	TUESDAY	WEDNESDAY
BREAKFAST:	BREAKFAST:	BREAKFAST:
LUNCH:	LUNCH:	LUNCH:
DINNER:	DINNER:	DINNER:
SNACKS:	SNACKS:	SNACKS:

My Notes For Meal Success!

THURSDAY	FRIDAY	SATURDAY	SUNDAY
BREAKFAST:	BREAKFAST:	BREAKFAST:	BREAKFAST:
LUNCH:	LUNCH:	LUNCH:	LUNCH:
DINNER:	DINNER:	DINNER:	DINNER:
SNACKS:	SNACKS:	SNACKS:	SNACKS:

NOTES:

My Notes For Meal Success!

Groceries

Produce

Meat

MONDAY	TUESDAY	WEDNESDAY
BREAKFAST:	BREAKFAST:	BREAKFAST:
LUNCH:	LUNCH:	LUNCH:
DINNER:	DINNER:	DINNER:
SNACKS:	SNACKS:	SNACKS:

My Notes For Meal Success!

THURSDAY	FRIDAY	SATURDAY	SUNDAY
BREAKFAST:	BREAKFAST:	BREAKFAST:	BREAKFAST:
LUNCH:	LUNCH:	LUNCH:	LUNCH:
DINNER:	DINNER:	DINNER:	DINNER:
SNACKS:	SNACKS:	SNACKS:	SNACKS:

NOTES:

My Notes For Meal Success!

Groceries

Produce

Meat

MONDAY	TUESDAY	WEDNESDAY
BREAKFAST:	BREAKFAST:	BREAKFAST:
LUNCH:	LUNCH:	LUNCH:
DINNER:	DINNER:	DINNER:
SNACKS:	SNACKS:	SNACKS:

My Notes For Meal Success!

THURSDAY	FRIDAY	SATURDAY	SUNDAY
BREAKFAST:	BREAKFAST:	BREAKFAST:	BREAKFAST:
LUNCH:	LUNCH:	LUNCH:	LUNCH:
DINNER:	DINNER:	DINNER:	DINNER:
SNACKS:	SNACKS:	SNACKS:	SNACKS:

NOTES:

My Notes For Meal Success!

Groceries

Produce

Meat

MONDAY	TUESDAY	WEDNESDAY
BREAKFAST:	BREAKFAST:	BREAKFAST:
LUNCH:	LUNCH:	LUNCH:
DINNER:	DINNER:	DINNER:
SNACKS:	SNACKS:	SNACKS:

My Notes For Meal Success!

THURSDAY	FRIDAY	SATURDAY	SUNDAY
BREAKFAST:	BREAKFAST:	BREAKFAST:	BREAKFAST:
LUNCH:	LUNCH:	LUNCH:	LUNCH:
DINNER:	DINNER:	DINNER:	DINNER:
SNACKS:	SNACKS:	SNACKS:	SNACKS:

NOTES:

My Notes For Meal Success!

Groceries

Produce

Meat

MONDAY	TUESDAY	WEDNESDAY
BREAKFAST:	BREAKFAST:	BREAKFAST:
LUNCH:	LUNCH:	LUNCH:
DINNER:	DINNER:	DINNER:
SNACKS:	SNACKS:	SNACKS:

My Notes For Meal Success!

THURSDAY	FRIDAY	SATURDAY	SUNDAY
BREAKFAST:	BREAKFAST:	BREAKFAST:	BREAKFAST:
LUNCH:	LUNCH:	LUNCH:	LUNCH:
DINNER:	DINNER:	DINNER:	DINNER:
SNACKS:	SNACKS:	SNACKS:	SNACKS:

NOTES:

My Notes For Meal Success!

Groceries

Produce

Meat

MONDAY	TUESDAY	WEDNESDAY
BREAKFAST:	BREAKFAST:	BREAKFAST:
LUNCH:	LUNCH:	LUNCH:
DINNER:	DINNER:	DINNER:
SNACKS:	SNACKS:	SNACKS:

My Notes For Meal Success!

THURSDAY	FRIDAY	SATURDAY	SUNDAY
BREAKFAST:	BREAKFAST:	BREAKFAST:	BREAKFAST:
LUNCH:	LUNCH:	LUNCH:	LUNCH:
DINNER:	DINNER:	DINNER:	DINNER:
SNACKS:	SNACKS:	SNACKS:	SNACKS:

NOTES:

My Notes For Meal Success!

Groceries

Produce

Meat

MONDAY	TUESDAY	WEDNESDAY
BREAKFAST:	BREAKFAST:	BREAKFAST:
LUNCH:	LUNCH:	LUNCH:
DINNER:	DINNER:	DINNER:
SNACKS:	SNACKS:	SNACKS:

My Notes For Meal Success!

THURSDAY	FRIDAY	SATURDAY	SUNDAY
BREAKFAST:	BREAKFAST:	BREAKFAST:	BREAKFAST:
LUNCH:	LUNCH:	LUNCH:	LUNCH:
DINNER:	DINNER:	DINNER:	DINNER:
SNACKS:	SNACKS:	SNACKS:	SNACKS:

NOTES:

My Notes For Meal Success!

Groceries

Produce

Meat

MONDAY	TUESDAY	WEDNESDAY
BREAKFAST:	BREAKFAST:	BREAKFAST:
LUNCH:	LUNCH:	LUNCH:
DINNER:	DINNER:	DINNER:
SNACKS:	SNACKS:	SNACKS:

My Notes For Meal Success!

THURSDAY	FRIDAY	SATURDAY	SUNDAY
BREAKFAST:	BREAKFAST:	BREAKFAST:	BREAKFAST:
LUNCH:	LUNCH:	LUNCH:	LUNCH:
DINNER:	DINNER:	DINNER:	DINNER:
SNACKS:	SNACKS:	SNACKS:	SNACKS:

NOTES:

My Notes For Meal Success!

Groceries

Produce

Meat

MONDAY	TUESDAY	WEDNESDAY
BREAKFAST:	BREAKFAST:	BREAKFAST:
LUNCH:	LUNCH:	LUNCH:
DINNER:	DINNER:	DINNER:
SNACKS:	SNACKS:	SNACKS:

My Notes For Meal Success!

THURSDAY	FRIDAY	SATURDAY	SUNDAY
BREAKFAST:	BREAKFAST:	BREAKFAST:	BREAKFAST:
LUNCH:	LUNCH:	LUNCH:	LUNCH:
DINNER:	DINNER:	DINNER:	DINNER:
SNACKS:	SNACKS:	SNACKS:	SNACKS:

NOTES:

My Notes For Meal Success!

Groceries

Produce

Meat

MONDAY	TUESDAY	WEDNESDAY
BREAKFAST:	BREAKFAST:	BREAKFAST:
LUNCH:	LUNCH:	LUNCH:
DINNER:	DINNER:	DINNER:
SNACKS:	SNACKS:	SNACKS:

My Notes For Meal Success!

THURSDAY	FRIDAY	SATURDAY	SUNDAY
BREAKFAST:	BREAKFAST:	BREAKFAST:	BREAKFAST:
LUNCH:	LUNCH:	LUNCH:	LUNCH:
DINNER:	DINNER:	DINNER:	DINNER:
SNACKS:	SNACKS:	SNACKS:	SNACKS:

NOTES:

My Notes For Meal Success!

Groceries

Produce

Meat

MONDAY	TUESDAY	WEDNESDAY
BREAKFAST:	BREAKFAST:	BREAKFAST:
LUNCH:	LUNCH:	LUNCH:
DINNER:	DINNER:	DINNER:
SNACKS:	SNACKS:	SNACKS:

My Notes For Meal Success!

	THURSDAY	FRIDAY	SATURDAY	SUNDAY
BREAKFAST:				
LUNCH:				
DINNER:				
SNACKS:				

NOTES:

www.ingramcontent.com/pod-product-compliance
Lightning Source LLC
Chambersburg PA
CBHW081311250726
48662CB00008B/2509

9 781683 265559